MIRAGES
AND OTHER MARVELS OF LIGHT AND AIR

BARBRA PENNE

Britannica®
Educational Publishing

IN ASSOCIATION WITH

ROSEN
EDUCATIONAL SERVICES

Published in 2017 by Britannica Educational Publishing (a trademark of Encyclopædia Britannica, Inc.) in association with The Rosen Publishing Group, Inc.
29 East 21st Street, New York, NY 10010

Distributed exclusively by Rosen Publishing.
To see additional Britannica Educational Publishing titles, go to rosenpublishing.com

First Edition

Britannica Educational Publishing
J.E. Luebering: Executive Director, Core Editorial
Mary Rose McCudden: Editor, Britannica Student Encyclopedia

Rosen Publishing
Shalini Saxena: Editor
Nelson Sá: Art Director
Michael Moy: Designer
Cindy Reiman: Photography Manager
Karen Huang: Photo Researcher

Library of Congress Cataloging-in-Publication Data

Names: Penne, Barbra, author.
Title: Mirages and other marvels of light and air / Barbra Penne.
Description: First edition. | New York : Britannica Educational Publishing in
  association with Rosen Educational Services, 2017. | 2017 | Series:
  Nature's mysteries | Audience: Grades 1 to 4. | Includes bibliographical
  references and index.
Identifiers: LCCN 2016000289| ISBN 9781680484816 (library bound : alk. paper)
  | ISBN 9781680484892 (pbk. : alk. paper) | ISBN 9781680484588 (6-pack :
  alk. paper)
Subjects: LCSH: Mirages—Juvenile literature. | Meteorological
  optics—Juvenile literature. | Light—Juvenile literature.
Classification: LCC QC976.M6 P46 2017 | DDC 551.56/5—dc23
LC record available at http://lccn.loc.gov/2016000289

Manufactured in the United States of America

Photo credits: Cover, p. 1 Jeremy Woodhouse/Photodisc/Getty Images; cover, p. 1 (cloudburst graphic) Macrovector/Shutterstock.com; p. 4 Frank Krahmer /DigitalVision/Getty Images; pp. 5, 16 Pete Turner/The Image Bank/Getty Images; p. 6 Driftwood/iStock/Thinkstock; pp. 7, 11, 12, 15, 19 Encyclopædia Britannica, Inc.; p. 8 Louise Murray/Science Source; p. 9 © Radius Images/Alamy Stock Photo; p. 10 Private Collection/© Look and Learn/Bridgeman Images; p. 13 Brocken Inaglory/Wikimedia Commons/File:Looming with towering and mirage of Farallon Islands.jpg/CC-BY-SA 3.0; p. 14 © david hancock/Alamy Stock Photo; p. 17 Private Collection/© Arthur Ackermann Ltd., London/Bridgeman Images; p. 18 Bob Chamberlin/Los Angeles Times/Getty Images; p. 20 Photos.com/Thinkstock; p. 21 Pekka Parviainen/Science Source; p. 22 A Rider/Science Source/Getty Images; p. 23 pincio/Shutterstock.com; p. 24 © jack stephens/Alamy Stock Photo; pp. 25, 27 Photo Researchers/Science Source/Getty Images; p. 26 Volcano Watch International-Stephen James O'Meara/National Geographic Image Collection/Getty Images; p. 28 Science & Society Picture Library/Getty Images; p. 29 © Andrzej Gorzkowski Photography/Alamy Stock Photo; interior pages background patterns Eky Studio /Shutterstock.com (rays), zffoto/Shutterstock.com (waves); back cover, interior pages background image kavram/Shutterstock.com.

CONTENTS

WHAT IS A MIRAGE?

Imagine this story. A lost traveler wanders through the desert. It is hot and dry. The traveler is very thirsty. Then he sees a pool of water ahead. He can't believe it. The traveler runs forward and tries to jump into the pool. But when he gets there, the water disappears. There is just sand below him. There was never any water. An image of water in the desert that really isn't there is one kind of mirage.

Some deserts have real pools of water like this one, but images of water in the desert are often mirages.

Mirages appear in many forms. A mirage is an image that looks real but is not truly there. Mirages are caused by layers of air being at different temperatures and **densities**. Cool air is denser than warm air. These properties can make light bend as it passes through the different layers. This bending, called refraction, creates images that trick your brain into believing an object is located where it is not.

The properties of the air in this desert cause the light to bend and form a mirage of a pool of water.

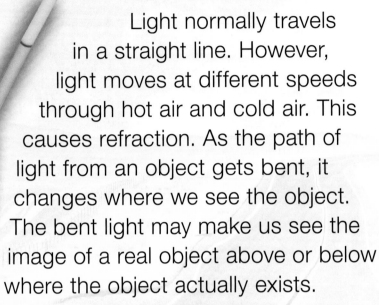

Light normally travels in a straight line. However, light moves at different speeds through hot air and cold air. This causes refraction. As the path of light from an object gets bent, it changes where we see the object. The bent light may make us see the image of a real object above or below where the object actually exists.

Mirages are illusions, not hallucinations. A hallucination is when the brain senses something that does not really exist. A hallucination is completely imagined by the brain. An illusion is different. It is something that

Refraction makes this straw appear bent at the surface of this drink.

looks or seems different from what it is, but it is a real image that can be seen and even photographed. The brain simply understands the illusion of a mirage image differently from how it really exists.

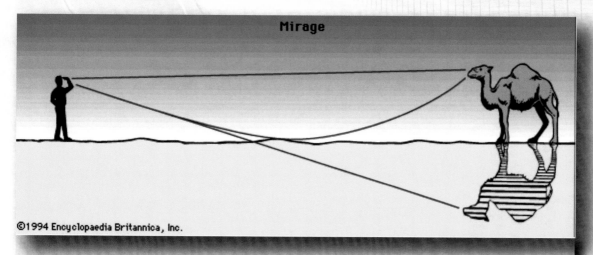

Mirage

©1994 Encyclopaedia Britannica, Inc.

When light rays are bent in unexpected ways, the brain can mis-understand them and see an object differently from how it truly exists.

WHERE DO MIRAGES HAPPEN?

Many mirages are seen around water or hot, flat surfaces. For example, ships may look like they're sailing upside down above the **horizon**. In reality these ships are beyond the horizon.

One of the most common examples of a mirage happens on highways during the summer. A shallow pool of water often seems to

Mirages often happen at the horizon, where distant objects may appear distorted or upside down.

VOCABULARY

The **horizon** is the line where the land or sea seems to meet the sky.

fill the road ahead. The reason for this false image is that a thin layer of heated air forms above the hot black pavement. This hot air meets the cooler air above. Light is bent, or refracted, where the layers of air meet. Light refracted from the blue sky looks like water on the ground. The "water" disappears as the observer approaches. A mirage similar to this one can lead people to think they are seeing a pool of water in the middle of a desert.

Mirages can be seen on hot summer pavement. If you came close to the "water" in this photo, it would simply disappear.

SUPERIOR MIRAGES

One type of mirage is called a superior mirage. In a superior mirage, an upside-down image of an object appears above where the object actually is. A well-known example of a superior mirage is a ship seen sailing upside down above the horizon. The real ship is often seen below the upside-down image. However, the actual ship may be out of sight below the horizon.

Fig. 14.—An Effect of Mirage observed by Captain Scoresby, while cruising off the Coast of Greenland in 1822.

In this superior mirage, upside-down images of ships float above the true ships.

Superior mirages happen when there is a layer of cool, dense air just above the surface of the water. The image reaches the person seeing it through this layer of air. Rays of light from the top of the ship are bent down more sharply than are rays from the bottom of the ship. This makes the image of the ship appear upside down.

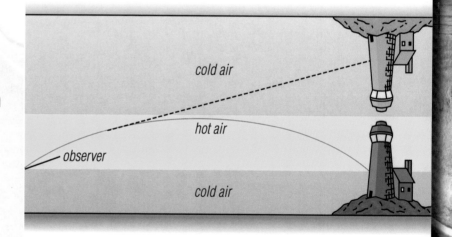

Formation of a Superior Image

cold air

hot air

observer

cold air

Light bends between cold and hot air to produce a superior mirage of an upside-down lighthouse above the real lighthouse.

LOOMING

Another type of illusion is called looming. Looming is similar to a superior mirage because an image appears above where the object really is. However, in looming, the image appears as the object truly is. It is not upside down.

Looming occurs when there is a layer of warm air above a layer of cool air. Light rays extending from an object

This diagram shows how looming works. The sailboat appears to be floating above where it truly is, but it is not upside down.

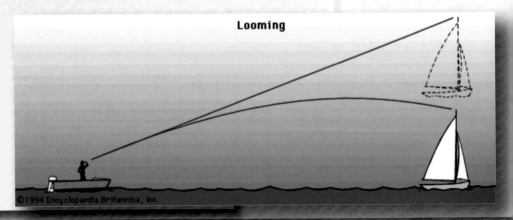

Looming

©1994 Encyclopaedia Britannica, Inc.

COMPARE AND CONTRAST

How are superior mirages and looming similar? What is the difference between the two?

in the cool layer are bent when they hit the warmer air. The light rays bend down and travel to an observer. The observer's brain thinks the light rays came from above so it tells the observer that the object is above. This makes it possible to see objects that are below the horizon. At such times, a boat below the horizon might appear as a right-side-up image that is floating in the sky.

Looming can also make it possible to see a distant shoreline that is normally too far to see, even in the clearest weather.

Sometimes, looming makes distant shorelines appear closer and larger, such as the islands in this photo.

INFERIOR MIRAGES

Probably the most common type of mirage is the inferior mirage. Inferior mirages are often seen in the summer over flat, hot surfaces. A car on the high-way ahead of you may look like it's driving through a shallow pool of water. You may even see a reflection of the car in the water.

Inferior mirages are caused by a thin layer of heated air that is close to the pavement. The heated air is less dense than the air above it. Light rays that reflect off the car and enter this heated

If a car on the road in the summer looks like it's reflected in a pool of water, it's most likely just an inferior mirage.

How are the conditions that cause superior mirages and inferior mirages different?

layer of air bend upward. An upside-down image of the car appears beneath the car. It seems to be a reflection of the car in a pool of water.

An inferior mirage and a superior mirage appear for opposite reasons. Remember the superior mirage of an upside-down ship sailing above the horizon. The superior mirage is caused by a layer of cool, dense air that hangs some distance above the surface of the water.

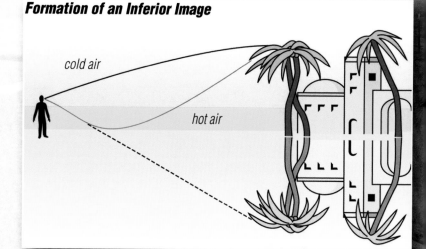

Formation of an Inferior Image

cold air

hot air

This diagram shows how light bends to produce an inferior mirage. The palace and trees appear upside down, below where they truly stand.

The mirage of water in the desert is also an inferior mirage. Inferior mirages are often seen in desert country where they appear as pools of water. This is because layers of air near the sand are hot. The "water" is simply the image of the blue sky appearing upside down below the line of sight. As the person seeing the mirage comes closer, the image disappears.

This inferior mirage is the source of popular and **exaggerated** desert stories. Many stories speak of desert oases with pools of water, palm trees, and

Mirages of water in the desert are actually inferior mirages in which the blue sky appears as a pool of water on the surface of the sand.

palaces. However, these are not realistic descriptions of mirages or of most actual oases.

An actual oasis is any area in a desert that has a supply of fresh water and where plants can therefore grow. It may be temporary or permanent, small or large. An oasis may appear as simple as a lone palm tree and a spring in the middle of a sandy desert.

Desert mirages have inspired popular tales, but often these stories are not realistic.

HEAT HAZE

Related to inferior mirages is heat haze. Heat haze describes the blurry, moving image of an object seen through heated air. An airport worker, standing on the runway, might see distant objects shimmering through the exhaust coming out of a plane engine. Somebody standing across from you at a barbecue might look blurry through the heated air above the grill's flames.

Heat haze happens because of unequally heated air between a person and an object they are seeing.

Heat haze caused by exhaust from a plane makes another plane appear blurry.

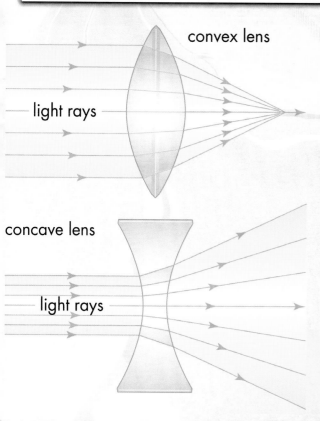

convex lens

light rays

concave lens

light rays

Moving layers of air act on light as **lenses** do. They bend the light rays that come from an object so the object appears distorted. "Heat devils" seen above hot radiators happen for the same reason. A heat devil is another name for the appearance of air shimmering above a heated surface.

This diagram shows how lenses bend light rays. Moving layers of air have a similar effect on rays of light.

FATA MORGANA

This illustration shows the sorceress Morgan le Fay casting a spell on Merlin the sorcerer.

The most famous mirage is one called the Fata Morgana. This mirage will sometimes appear over a body of water called the Strait of Messina between Italy and Sicily. It is named after the **legendary** sorceress Morgan le Fay, who appears in many stories about King Arthur. The Fata Morgana takes the form of weird castles that rise from the sea and change their shape. The castles may rise into the air or become squished into a thin line.

The Fata Morgana is a complex mirage. It is probably the result of looming and a mix of superior and inferior images. Changing layers of air change the image of the cliffs and houses on the opposite shore and make them bigger. The houses appear to become the legendary castles of Morgan le Fay.

The name "Fata Morgana" is now used for a type of mirage that looks like islands and other stretched-out or floating objects in the sea.

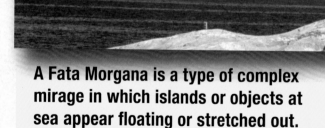

A Fata Morgana is a type of complex mirage in which islands or objects at sea appear floating or stretched out.

MIRAGES HIGH IN THE SKY

The refracted part of the setting Sun blends with the rest of the Sun's image. It looks like an Etruscan vase.

Mirages don't only happen when viewing objects that are in our atmosphere. Mirages can also occur when we view objects from Earth that are in space. Such mirages are usually visible during sunrises and sunsets. Mirages in Earth's sky may also take place when viewing the Moon and other visible planets in our solar system.

Most often, an inferior mirage is what is taking place in the sky. Hot air near Earth's surface makes the Sun appear distorted as it sets. However, because the Sun is so big, a person watching the sunset will see some parts of the Sun directly while other parts are refracted.

Some phases of a sunset mirage have names based on the shape of the Sun's image. Early in a sunset mirage, the Sun looks like an **Etruscan vase**. While the Sun is still mostly above the horizon, its bottom edge is refracted. This upside-down image blends with the rest of the Sun's image. The refracted part looks like a vase's base.

The shape of this Etruscan vase is similar to that of many sunset mirages.

As sunset continues, the top part of the image gets smaller. At the same time, the base grows larger. The Sun slowly begins to look like the capital Greek letter omega (Ω). Eventually, the Sun looks like a thin disc before setting.

Another mirage made by the Sun's image is the Novaya Zemlya effect. (Novaya Zemlya is a group of islands in Russia where this type of mirage was first seen.) This mirage lets people see the Sun rising before it has actually reached the horizon.

Sometimes, complex "mock

The Novaya Zemlya effect lets a person see the Sun rising before it has actually come up or continue to see the Sun after it has already set.

mirages" happen when viewing the Sun, the Moon, or other planets in Earth's sky. In a mock mirage, several different images can be produced. The Sun might seem cut up into layers or flat like a pancake.

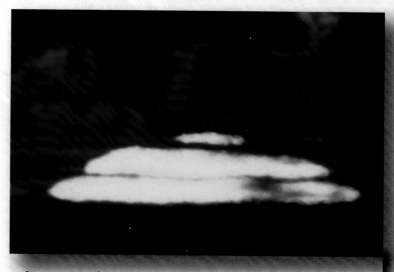

In a complex mirage, the Sun may look flattened out or cut up into layers, as it appears here.

GREEN FLASHES

Sometimes an effect called a green flash can be seen during a sunset. A green flash happens just as the Sun moves below the horizon. For one short moment, a bright green ray of light appears at the top of the Sun.

Whenever light is refracted, it can create different colors. Mirages are seen when Earth's atmosphere acts like a

Just before the Sun sets, it sometimes creates a bright green flash, as seen in the lower two photos of this setting Sun.

prism. Green flashes are simply another effect of light being refracted as it passes through the atmosphere. In the case of this mirage, the Sun's image becomes magnified. Its magnification helps somebody watching the sunset see the green edge, or green flash, without binoculars or a telescope. Green flashes are difficult to see.

Green flashes can also be seen during sunrise. Then, the green flash appears just before the Sun rises above the horizon. Sometimes, if the air is clear, a blue flash can also be seen during a sunrise or sunset.

While less common, sometimes a setting or rising Sun can also create a blue flash, such as this one.

WILL-O'-THE-WISPS AND OTHER UNEXPLAINED LIGHTS

A will-o'-the-wisp is a mysterious light often seen at night flickering over marshes. When approached, it moves away. In some places it is called a jack-o'-lantern. In popular legend they are considered a bad sign.

There is no certain explanation of will-o'-the-wisps. Some scientists believe they happen

The mysterious will-o'-the-wisp is an unexplained type of light that often appears floating over marshes.

THINK ABOUT IT

Marfa, Texas, is in the desert. Knowing what we've learned about mirages, how could car headlights appear to be floating in the sky above where they truly are?

when marsh gases catch fire. (Marsh gases are mostly made up of methane, a gas that catches fire easily.)

Other unexplained lights appear regularly on clear nights in the town of Marfa, Texas. The twinkling lights appear at a distance, sometimes as colored light. They float in the air, split in two, come together, or hover. Some people believe they are just headlights from a nearby highway. Others believe they are caused by the refraction of light as it passes through the air.

This road sign points the way to an area where viewers can watch the mystery lights of Marfa, Texas.

GLOSSARY

ATMOSPHERE The whole mass of air surrounding Earth.

BINOCULARS A handheld device that magnifies faraway objects to make them easier to see.

COMPLEX Composed of two or more parts.

DENSITY How close together or compact the particles that make up a substance are.

DISTORTED Twisted out of a natural, normal, or original shape or appearance.

FLICKERING Moving irregularly or unsteadily.

INVERTED Turned upside down.

MAGNIFIED Larger in appearance.

METHANE A colorless gas that has no smell and that can be burned for fuel.

MOCK Not real; make-believe.

PHASES Parts or steps in a process or series of related events.

REFLECTION The bouncing of light off of a surface.

REFRACTION The bending of a light as it passes from one medium into another.

SORCERESS A female witch.

TELESCOPE A device shaped like a long tube that you look through in order to see things that are far away.

FOR MORE INFORMATION

Books

Greek, Joe. *What Is the Atmosphere?* New York, NY: Britannica Educational Publishing, 2015.

Jacobson, Ryan. *Step-by-Step Experiments with Light and Vision*. Mankato, MN: The Child's World, 2012.

Kuskowski, Alex. *Science Experiments with Light*. Minneapolis, MN: ABDO, 2014.

Manolis, Kay. *Density*. Minneapolis, MN: Bellwether Media, 2009.

Riley, Peter D. *Flash! Light and How We See Things*. London, England: Franklin Watts, 2012.

Rooney, Anne. *Optical Engineering and the Science of Light*. St. Catharines, ON, Canada: Crabtree Publishing, 2014.

Websites

Because of the changing nature of Internet links, Rosen Publishing has developed an online list of websites related to the subject of this book. This site is updated regularly. Please use this link to access this list:

http://www.rosenlinks.com/NMY/mira

INDEX